Special Publication 90   1992

Site Safety

a handbook for young construction professionals

prepared by

S C Bielby

BTech (Hons) CEng MICE MIOSH

Scott Wilson Kirkpatrick & Partners

 Construction Industry Research and Information Association
6 Storey's Gate, Westminster, London SW1P 3AU
Tel: 071-222 8891   Fax: 071-222 1708

A half of all the people who die on a construction site have been working there for less than two weeks.

70% of fatal construction accidents could have been prevented by effective management action.

Foreword

This handbook has been prepared in response to mounting concerns expressed by all sides of the construction industry about the hazards of building and civil engineering work in general, and the very real risks to health and safety faced by young construction professionals in particular.

'Site Safety' aims to alert young professionals – including engineers, architects and surveyors – to the hazards they will meet on a day-to-day basis. It is an easy-to-use ready reference guide which summarises the main aspects of site health and safety and the steps which young professionals should take to make construction sites safer for themselves and all others who work on them. Young people who are just starting their careers are particularly vulnerable to accidents and I would urge them to read this handbook and follow the advice which it contains.

I particularly welcome the fact that, through CIRIA, all sides of the construction industry have been involved in producing this handbook, together with HSE's Technology and Health Sciences Division. I see its publication as a helpful step towards reducing the level of accidents in this sector and commend it to all young professionals.

John Cullen.

Sir John Cullen
Chairman
Health and Safety Commission

London
July 1992

Summary

Building and civil engineering construction sites contain many hazards. The risks to young professionals – engineers, architects and surveyors – going to work on them for the first time is very considerable.

The "Site Safety handbook" has been prepared to alert young professionals to the more common hazards present on site, to advise them on safer construction practices for themselves and others, and to help them manage these very important responsibilities.

Although the text is written in the context of the legal framework provided by the Health and Safety at Work etc Act of 1974, the handbook is *not a legal document nor a comprehensive manual* to site safety. These already exist, but because of their bulk generally stay within site offices.

The handbook is designed to be an easy-to-read ready reference guide for use outside, which will slip easily into a pocket. To achieve its purpose, the text has been kept brief.

The text is divided into three main parts:

- **"Before going on site"** – three chapters explain the responsibilities of the young professional and the preparations needed before going on site
- **"Site activities and hazards"** – this part contains 25 chapters each dealing with a principal risk, eg falling, temporary works
- **"Your contribution"** – three chapters explain what the young professional should do to deal with hazards, assist with accidents and what to do to investigate them.

It ends with a reference section and an index.

The handbook starts with a Foreword by Sir John Cullen, Chairman of the Health and Safety Commission.

Summary

Site Safety handbook
Construction Industry Research and Information Association
Special Publication 90, London 1992

Keywords:	construction site, health and safety, risks, hazards, law, young professional, personal preparation, protective equipment, accidents, working practices, training, safety legislation, management, precautions.
Reader interest:	young construction professionals - engineers, architects, surveyors, planners; clients; consultants; local authorities; safety officers; students; site managers.

First published 1992, reprinted 1993
© CIRIA 1992   ISBN 0 86017 358 5

CLASSIFICATION

Availability	Unrestricted
Content	Advice/guidance
Status	Committee guided
User	Construction professionals and managers

Published by CIRIA, 6 Storey's Gate, Westminster, London, SW1P 3AU

Acknowledgements

Concept

The Site Safety handbook is the outcome of CIRIA Research Project 447. The need for the handbook was first identified by CIRIA's former Advisory Committee on Construction Operations.

Research Contractor

The work was undertaken by Scott Wilson Kirkpatrick and Partners, Consulting Engineers under contract to CIRIA.

The Project Supervisor was Mr P A Green BSc FCGI FGS FICE FIHT MConsE, Partner.
The Technical Author was Mr S C Bielby BTech(Hons) C.Eng, MICE, MIOSH, Principal Engineer.
The Graphic Designer and Coordinator was Ms L Baxendale BA(Hons).

Copyright

CIRIA is grateful to the following organisations for permission to reproduce their material in the handbook:

HMSO
CITB
RoSPA
V J Davies
Tiefbau - Berufsgenossenschaft.

Financial Contributions

The project was undertaken as part of CIRIA's Core Research Programme. Core Programme members are listed on the inside back cover. The following water services plcs supported the work financially:

North West Water
Southern Water
Thames Water
Wessex Water
Yorkshire Water.

Acknowledgements

Project Steering Group

CIRIA and Scott Wilson Kirkpatrick wish to express their appreciation to the Project Steering Group which guided the work and agreed the text. It comprised:

D E Wright (Chairman)
DIC PhD FICE MIWEM MASCE — Applied Research and Project Management Services

J M Anderson BA BSc ARCST CEng MICE FGS — Health and Safety Executive

M J Barnard BEng CEng MICE MIOSH RSP — Travers Morgan Ltd

D F Bishop FIOSH RSP AIIM — Costain Group

J F Davey MSc CEng MICE MIStructE — Ove Arup Partnership

V J Davies CEng FICE — Consulting Engineer (representing ICE Safety Panel)

J Y Dutton BSc CEng FICE MBIM — Consulting Engineer

R A Forster MIOSH — Galliford plc

F G W Gaugain MIOSH ACIOB — Balfour Beatty Ltd

C A Loveridge CEng BTech MICE — Thames Water Utilities Ltd

R Lucas MIOSH MIIRSM AFRM — AMEC plc

J H Phipps — Sir Robert McAlpine Ltd

J A Read CEng MICE MIOSH — W S Atkins Limited

C B Tisi FIOSH RSP — Wimpey Group Services Ltd

J H O Williams CEng MICE MIWEM — Babcock Water Engineering Ltd

D A Wrennall BEng(Hons) — Tarmac Construction Ltd (and representing ICE AMGS Committee)

R F Bell BSc (Eng) CEng FICE — Consultant CIRIA.

The text went through may revisions. Comments on the first substantive draft were collated and edited by Mr V J Davies, Mr J Y Dutton, Mr R A Forster and Mr J A Read, each of whom spent considerable time on this onerous task.

Source materials

CIRIA is grateful to the following organisations which made their company documents on safety available for reference by Scott Wilson Kirkpatrick:

Ove Arup Partnership
W S Atkins Limited
Balfour Beatty Ltd
Building Employers Confederation
Construction Industry Training Board
Costain Group
Health and Safety Executive

HMSO
Institution of Civil Engineers
Royal Institution of Chartered Surveyors
Thames Water Utilities Ltd
Travers Morgan Ltd.

Contents

Contents

Starting Point

Young professionals!

Did you realise that every other working day (on average) someone dies on a British construction site? – and that is something that legislation alone cannot change. This handbook is essential reading when you go on site, regardless of your job description. It is directly relevant to all young construction professionals, including:

- civil engineers
- structural engineers
- architects
- quantity surveyors
- H&V engineers

- planners
- electrical engineers
- mechanical engineers
- building engineers
- surveyors.

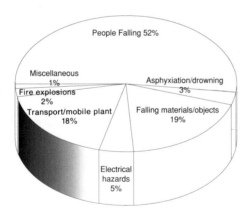

The major causes of construction deaths

People Falling 52%
Miscellaneous 1%
Fire explosions 2%
Transport/mobile plant 18%
Asphyxiation/drowning 3%
Falling materials/objects 19%
Electrical hazards 5%

You have a 1 in 2 chance of injury during 20 years working on site.

Scope of the handbook

This handbook has been designed as a ready reference guide to advise you about health and safety and to help you understand and manage health and safety in construction. *However it is not a legal document nor a comprehensive manual.*

It highlights the common hazards that you will be meeting on a day-to-day basis. It promotes safer construction practices by dealing with basic safety standards that you will need to apply on construction sites. The handbook does not cover ionising radiation, compressed air, explosives, quarrying, diving, tunnelling or other specialist activities which you are unlikely to encounter during your early days on site. Specialist training is required for these activities before you go on such sites.

The handbook is in four main sections:

- Before going on site
- Site activities and hazards
- Your contribution
- Further help and information.

The section on 'Site activities and hazards' consists of 25 brief chapters arranged in alphabetical order. The figures illustrate a basic safety point, but are not definitive working drawings.

It slips easily into your pocket so that it is at hand wherever and whenever you need it. This book could help save your life... or the life of one of your colleagues. This handbook has been written for you... because safety on site is something you cannot afford to ignore, and **you** have statutory responsibilities for safety.

1.1 Your Responsibilities

You must work within this framework to manage health and safety:

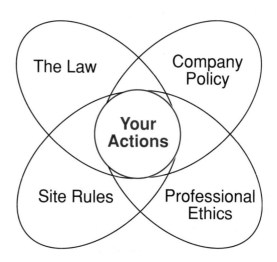

Health and safety is an integral part of the responsibilities of everyone on site and must be exercised within a management framework. This includes:

- legal requirements
- your own company policy and its implementation
- specific site rules for safe systems of work
- professional codes of conduct and ethics.

As a professional, you can play an important part in helping to encourage safer construction practices and to prevent dangerous acts which could lead to accidents.

Within the European Community (EC) there are 8000 industrial deaths each year.

The Law

If there is a conflict between statute law, contract requirements, company policy, site rules or professional ethics, then safety legislation takes precedence.

The Health and Safety at Work etc. Act 1974 provides a comprehensive legislative framework to promote, stimulate and encourage high standards of health and safety in the work place. The aim of the Act is to increase health and safety awareness and to promote effective standards in every organisation.

Everyone is involved: management, employees, self-employed, employees' representatives, those in charge of premises and the manufacturers of plant, equipment, substances and materials in matters of health and safety. The Act also deals with the protection of the public, where they may be affected by the activities of people at work.

The Act consists of four Parts, but only Part 1 directly concerns you.

The main provisions of Part 1 of the Act include:

- to secure the health, safety and welfare of persons at work
- to protect persons other than persons at work against risks to health and safety arising out of, or in connection with, the activities of persons at work
- to control the keeping and use of explosive or highly flammable or otherwise dangerous substances
- to control the emission into the atmosphere of noxious or offensive substances
- to provide for criminal offences and punishments.

The Act established a Health and Safety Commission and Executive to enforce and administer the Act and the Regulations made under it.

1.3 Your Responsibilities

The Act says that your responsibilities are:

a) to take reasonable care for the health and safety of yourself and others who may be affected by your acts or omissions at work; and

b) to co-operate with your employer and any other person properly involved in all matters relating to health and safety law and any duty or requirement that the employer may be required to make under that law.

It is also an offence for any person intentionally or recklessly to interfere with or misuse anything provided in the interests of health, safety or welfare that the law may require.

Other Acts and Regulations which you will need to understand as your career progresses currently include:

- Construction (General Provisions) Regulations
- Construction (Health and Welfare) Regulations
- Construction (Lifting Operations) Regulations
- Construction (Working Places) Regulations
- Construction (Head Protection) Regulations
- The Control Of Substances Hazardous to Health (COSHH) Regulations
- The Noise at Work Regulations
- The Electricity at Work Regulations.

Consult the Construction Safety manual for a complete list of Acts and Regulations relevant to construction. Note that these will be amended from time to time.

Company policy and its implementation

Every employer with five or more employees is required to provide a written statement of his general policy, organisation and arrangements for health and safety at work, to show or give this to all employees, and to keep it up to date.

A statement of company safety policy will explain:

- what your employer intends should happen
- how the employer is going to set up and maintain a safe and healthy working environment
- what health and safety responsibilities exist
- who is responsible and how to contact them
- that safe systems of work exist and who is responsible for them
- the arrangements for review and update etc.

You must read this policy, understand your responsibilities and carry them out.

It is important that you know the organisational structure and who you should ask for health and safety advice. Normally this will be your manager or the appointed safety advisor/ supervisor for your site.

Site rules for safe systems of work

Every site is unique and requires specific rules for safe systems of working. These should be contained in written method statements, which should cover all hazardous operations, including:

- frame erecting
- roofing
- cladding
- painting at height
- demolishing structures
- hot working
- scaffolding
- working in confined spaces
- removing asbestos
- excavating
- pressure testing
- working over water.

1.5 Your Responsibilities

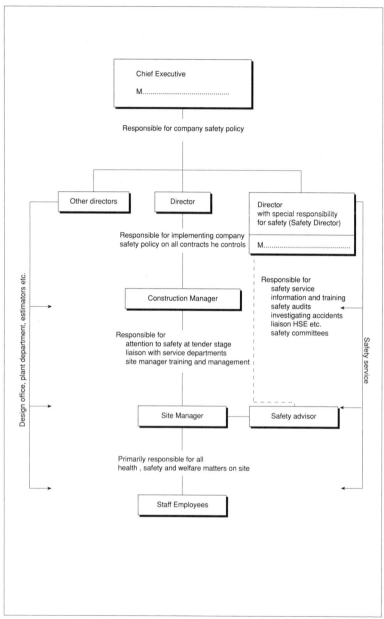

**Responsibilities for health and safety
in a typical company**

The method statement will typically include information on:

- the person in charge of operations
- safe means of access to all work areas
- specific details of any lifting appliances, including positioning on site and lifting gear to be used
- details of storage of materials and methods for dealing with hazardous substances
- how the work is to be carried out, covering items such as slinging points, the programme of work and exact details on work progression (eg start, grid line, direction of work etc.)
- communications
- the equipment to be used
- protective clothing and equipment to be worn.

No deviation from the method statement should be allowed without referring back to the writer of the method statement and a revised statement being produced.

Professional codes of conduct

All members of professional bodies are bound by their code of conduct. For example, item 1 of the Rules for Professional Conduct of the ICE state that:

"A member, in his responsibility to his employer and to the profession, shall have full regard to the public interest, particularly in matters of health and safety."

Other Institutions have similar rules.

Method statements must be issued and explained to the people carrying out the work. Their understanding of the statements must be confirmed.

1.7 Your Responsibilities

Your Actions

If you see a situation which, in your opinion, involves a risk of death or serious injury, you have a **duty** and a right to take immediate action.

This includes one or more of the following actions:

- tell the person in danger to stop, explaining why – but don't put yourself at risk
- contact the person in charge of the activity and your immediate manager and inform them of your actions
- later inform appropriate senior site personnel
- if you are uncertain about the degree of risk involved, consult your immediate manager before taking any **further** action.

If you ignore a danger you condone it and will share responsibility for any accident. Do not be put off or let yourself be overridden if you believe the danger is there. Things that look unsafe usually are.

Other risks should be dealt with through your formal channels of communication – refer the matter to your manager and your safety advisor. The HSE seeks to provide advice and guidance on health and safety matters. Consult them if you cannot get advice within your own organisation.

If in doubt, ask your immediate manager without delay.

2.1 Getting Ready

Think ahead – what will you be doing on site?

Then:

- find out about relevant legislation and the standards it requires you to follow
- check your company policy statement and local arrangements and think how you will comply with them
- read relevant method statements
- obtain the necessary equipment, protective clothing and materials
- make sure you understand company working practices
- evaluate your need for further training.

On joining a new site, you should:

- report to the site office and read the site notices
- discuss your previous safety training/experience (if any) with your immediate manager
- read the company safety policy and have the safety organisation explained
- be given induction training, including site safety rules and method statements, and receive instructions in safety procedures
- be given the name and location of the safety adviser
- be informed of the need to use protective clothing and equipment
- bring with you your safety equipment
- be told of your personal responsibilities for health and safety
- have explained to you the authorisation necessary for the use of plant, machinery, powered hand tools, etc
- be told how to report near misses and defective plant and equipment

See also
Chapter 3

- see the first aid facilities
- see the site and discuss its hazards.

Discuss these points with your manager or safety adviser to ensure you understand them.

You will also need to inform your manager of any illness or disability which may affect your site actions, eg colour blindness, epilepsy, diabetes or vertigo.

You must not come to work under the influence of alcohol or drugs or take alcohol or drugs while at work.

Avoid working alone until you know the site layout. If you must work alone ALWAYS tell your immediate supervisor:

- where you are going
- what you will be doing
- when you will be back
- that you **are** back.

Wear appropriate clothing, particularly footwear, helmet and high visibility clothing and tie back long hair so that it doesn't get trapped in moving parts or machinery.

 You are most at risk during your first days on site. Think – and plan ahead.

3.1 Personal Protective Equipment

Personal Protective Equipment (PPE) does not stop accidents, but it can help to lessen their effects. Employers have a duty to eliminate the hazard and/or control the risk, so far as is reasonably practicable. PPE therefore represents a last line of defence for the individual.

There are many types of PPE from helmets to footwear, each type designed to protect different parts of the body against specific hazards. This chapter explains some of the common types of PPE.

Everyone issued with suitable protective clothing or equipment should be told:

- how to wear and use it
- the hazards against which it affords protection
- the limitations of the protection
- how to maintain and store it
- how to keep it clean
- to report loss, damage or deterioration immediately it is detected (including the person to report to) and to obtain replacements
- to report any problems in its use
- when to return for replacement items with a limited life
- to sign for receipt of issue and any replacement.

In addition to the equipment intended for specific hazards, there is of course general protective clothing for work in wet and cold weather, and high visibility clothing for roadworks.

 Over 4,000 head injuries sustained at work were reported in Britain in 1990/91.

Personal Protective Equipment 3.2

Head protection

The Construction (Head Protection) Regulations 1989 require that head protection is worn when directed to do so, or to comply with written site rules.

Change your helmet:

- at the manufacturers recommended frequency or
- after a significant impact or
- if it becomes deeply scratched or cracked.

Do not leave your helmet in bright sunlight – this weakens the plastic.

Foot and leg protection

Safety footwear with both toe and sole reinforcement is essential on site to prevent crush injuries to your toes and to stop sharp objects puncturing the soles of your feet.

Over 40,000 foot, ankle and leg injuries sustained at work were reported in Britain in 1990/91.

3.3 Personal Protective Equipment

Hearing protection

Regular exposure to excessive noise causes damage to the inner ear and permanent loss of hearing. A single exposure to a very loud noise can have the same effect. Many types of ear defenders are available from disposable ear plugs to ear muffs and system helmets incorporating ear defenders and suitable protection can be found for every situation - WEAR IT.

There will be occasions when you will be legally required to wear ear protection and may be prosecuted if you fail to do so.

Eye protection

There are several types of eye protectors and it is important to wear the correct type to give the required protection.

Seek advice from your safety adviser about the eye protection you will need and only use if for the specified purpose.

Over 4,000 eye injuries sustained at work were reported in Britain in 1990/91.

See also
Chapter 17

Hand and arm protection

Gloves give protection against cuts, toxic or irritant chemicals and dermatitis, eg that caused by cement. Use barrier creams and always check you have the correct gloves to protect against the particular hazard you face. Always wash your hands before eating, drinking or smoking.

Respiratory protection

There is a wide choice of respiratory protection for dusts, gases and bacteria. Seek advice from your safety adviser on the appropriate type for a job. Use respiratory protection in accordance with a written method statement for a safe system of work.

Special protection

Careful selection, maintenance, certification and regular training are needed for specialist equipment including:

- compressed air escape breathing apparatus
- artificial respirators
- fall arrester and safety harnesses.

Always select these with your manager or safety adviser and ensure written safe systems of work are followed.

Wear your personal protective equipment.

4.1 Access/Egress

People and vehicular access should be separated when ever possible

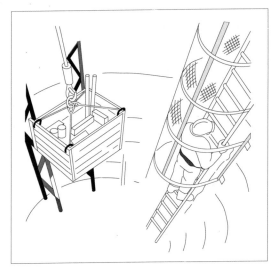

Safe access for people and their tools, equipment and materials must be provided

A labourer fell 3m to his death while trying to use a roof as an unauthorised access route to a scaffold.

See also
Chapters 8, 13 & 19

Ground level access/egress - follow these rules:

- all visitors (including those making deliveries) should report direct to a site access control point
- access for pedestrians and vehicles should be separated wherever possible
- pedestrian refuges must be used where provided
- adequate lighting and signs should be provided on all access routes
- access routes must be kept free of obstructions and tripping hazards.

Access/egress above ground level

Safe access to heights must be provided by use of ladders, passenger hoists or lifts which are:

- sited away from the danger of vehicle impact
- on a stable foundation
- designed, erected, inspected and maintained by competent people.

Gangways and runways must be:

- at least 3 boards wide if used only by people
- at least 5 boards wide if used for materials access
- provided with guard rails and toe boards
- less than 1 in $1^1/_2$ slope.

Safety lines, harnesses, cradles and bosun's chairs should only be used by trained personnel in conjunction with a written method statement for the work, which must include fixing point details.

5.1 Bottled Gases

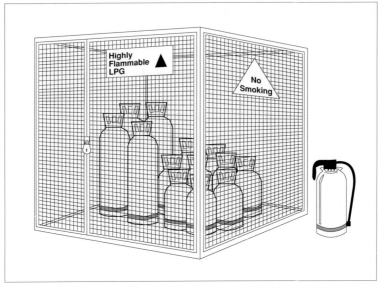

Store LPG outside in a secure well ventilated area.

When LPG is used a fire extinguisher must always be available at the worksite. Staff must be instructed in emergency procedures

Bottled gases used on construction site include:

- liquified petroleum gas (LPG)
- oxygen
- acetylene.

All will cause fires and explosions if misused.

Always observe No Smoking signs and procedures.

A mobile bitumen boiler overturned and set fire to two propane cylinders which exploded, killing a 12 year old who was playing nearby.

See also Chapter 14

You should be aware of the following safe working practices for storage, use and transport.

Storage:

- store cylinders upright in secure well ventilated labelled cages or purpose-built containers
- provide fire extinguishers nearby
- separate full and empty cylinders
- separate flammable gases from oxygen (minimum 3m)
- site the storage cage away from buildings and excavations
- never store cylinders below ground level or in confined spaces
- never store or use an LPG cylinder in a site hut.

Use:

- ensure that cylinders are upright and cannot be easily knocked over
- check hoses, couplings and regulator for wear or damage, and ensure that flash-back arresters are used
- follow manufacturers' instructions
- always provide good ventilation
- keep bitumen boilers or similar at least 3m from the cylinders
- return cylinders to the approved store at the end of work.

Transport:

- transport cylinders on open or well-ventilated vehicles
- secure the cylinders in an upright position
- carry an appropriate fire extinguisher
- display statutory warning notices
- ensure that drivers are trained and instructed in the hazards of carrying bottled gases.

6.1 Building Maintenance

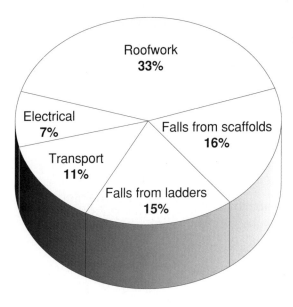

Roofwork
33%

Electrical
7%

Falls from scaffolds
16%

Transport
11%

Falls from ladders
15%

The five main
causes of
fatalities which
occur during
maintenance
work.

 Over 40% of all construction fatalities occur
during maintenance work.

See also
Chapters 11, 13, 19 & 28

It is essential that maintenance work is planned and executed with the same professionalism as major works. The five major causes of deaths are shown on the pie chart opposite.

Everyone involved in maintenance work must understand the hazards and the correct procedures to minimise risk. A permit to work may be required for:

- entry into confined spaces or plant and machinery
- hot work which may cause explosion or fires
- work on pipework carrying hazardous substances
- mechanical or electrical work requiring isolation of power
- roofwork over a production line
- excavation work within a factory area
- work with asbestos.

Lock off devices must be used to isolate the power supply. They must be locked off before carrying out maintenance work on or near plant and machinery, etc. Permit-to-work systems must be controlled by an authorised person.

Structural stability should always be considered during maintenance and alternative means of support provided when normal supports are removed.

Remember:
- **plan the work and consider its impact on people nearby**
- **provide safe access, egress and working places**
- **use lock-off devices**
- **initiate permit-to-work systems**
- **it only takes an instant to be injured**
- **do not work alone unless it is necessary.**

7.1 Chemicals, Dust and Fumes

Inflammable liquids	Compressed gases	Oxidising substances
Inflammable solids	Radioactive material	Poisonous substances
Organic peroxides	Spontaneously combustible substances	Corrosive substances
Toxic gases	Substances which are dangerous when wet	Inflammable gases

The hazard diamonds illustrated above tell you the nature of the hazard of a substance. They appear on bulk tankers and on fixed installations, eg storerooms and on packaging and containers.

Chemicals, dust and fumes can enter your body in 3 ways:

- by inhalation
- by swallowing
- through the skin.

The effects may be immediate or may only appear after several years.

The Control of Substances Hazardous to Health (COSHH) Regulations are aimed at the protection of workers from the effects of hazardous substances. Hazardous substances include:

- solvents
- cement
- glues
- plaster
- weedkiller
- bitumen
- fillers
- brick dust
- silica dust
- toxic substances in the ground, eg PCBs (chemicals found in electrical equipment).

The COSHH regulations require 6 steps to be taken by employers:

- know the substances employees (including you) may be exposed to
- assess the hazard to health they can cause
  - level of risk
  - degree of exposure
- eliminate or control the hazard
  - use a non hazardous alternative
  - limit the number of people exposed to the substance
- inform, instruct and train employees in
  - the nature of the risk
  - control measures to adopt
  - reasons for using PPE
  - monitoring to be carried out
- monitor the effectiveness of controls and initiate health surveillance where appropriate
- keep records.

Remember that a COSHH assessment considers the work process, the substances involved, the risks to health and safety, who is involved and how the substance could cause harm, eg by skin contact.

7.3 Chemicals, Dust and Fumes

These symbols appear on packaging and containers to warn of the hazards associated with their contents:

Meaning

Safety Precautions and Medical Action

Toxic/Very Toxic

May cause serious health risk or even death if inhaled, ingested or penetrates the skin

1. Wear suitable protective clothing, gloves and eye/face protection.
2. After contact with skin, wash immediately with plenty of water.
3. In case of contact with eyes, rinse immediately with plenty of water and seek medical advice.
4. In case of accident or if you feel unwell, seek medical advice immediately.

Corrosive

On contact may cause destruction of living tissue or burns

1. Wear suitable gloves and eye/face protection.
2. Take off immediately all contaminated clothing.
3. In case of contact with skin, wash immediately with plenty of water.
4. In case of contact with eyes, rinse immediately with plenty of water and seek medical advice.

Harmful

May cause limited health risk if inhaled, ingested or penetrates the skin

1. Do not breathe vapour / spray / dust.
2. Avoid contact with skin.
3. Wash thoroughly before you eat, drink or smoke.
4. In case of contact with eyes, rinse immediately with plenty of water and seek medical advice.

Irritant

May cause inflammation or irritation on immediate, repeated or prolonged contact with the skin, or if inhaled

1. Do not breathe vapour / spray / dust.
2. Avoid contact with skin.
3. In case of contact with eyes, rinse immediately with plenty of water and seek medical advice.
4. In case of contact with skin, wash immediately with plenty of water.

Highly Flammable

May become hot or catch fire in contact with air or is gaseous and will ignite at any ignition source

1. Protect from source of ignition
2. Have fire precautions at hand

Some substances can poison you by being directly absorbed through the skin, while others cause skin problems, eg dermatitis. Dust particles entering your lungs cause scarring of the lung tissue and many cause cancer. Fumes can be fatal, especially in poorly ventilated areas. Safe systems of work must be used to limit the amount of dust and fumes produced and to limit skin contact with hazardous chemicals.

Your duties under COSHH are to:

- take part in training programmes
- read container labels and COSHH information sheets
- follow safe working practices and method statements
- use the correct PPE
- pay attention to personal hygiene
- store chemicals and equipment safely
- report any hazard or defect to your manager
- take part in health surveillance
- know emergency procedures.

You should be aware of the risks to third parties posed by legitimate activities, or accidents, occurring within the site, for example, wind blown paint spray or dust, or accidental pollution of rivers and drains.

Two common site hazards, **lead** and **asbestos**, are not covered by COSHH as they have their own specific regulations. The points outlined above, however, still hold true.

> **The COSHH Regulations require the identification and control of ALL hazardous substances at work.**

8.1 Confined Spaces

Confined spaces can kill.

Two cases illustrate the point:

> At a reservoir site four men, all aged under 30 and physically fit, died in a surface water manhole 4m deep. Naturally evolved carbon dioxide had displaced oxygen. No tests were made before entry. The first man down collapsed and the three other men climbed down to their deaths in futile attempts to effect a rescue.

> When an engineer collapsed in a sewer, a rescuer entered without breathing apparatus and was overcome; a second person made a similar vain attempt to reach the victims. When the rescue team from the fire brigade arrived they had to remove the two would-be rescuers before they could get to the engineer. By that time it was too late and he died.

Typical confined spaces include:

- shafts
- tunnels
- man holes
- sewers
- box girders
- ceiling voids
- cellars and basements
- boilers and process vessels.

Confined spaces are **not** necessarily small.

If in doubt, assume the workplace is a confined space.

Confined spaces are subject to 3 main hazards:

- suffocation – lack of oxygen
- toxic atmosphere – presence or ingress of gases
  eg carbon monoxide
      hydrogen sulphide
      nitrogen oxides
- flammable atmosphere – presence or ingress of gases
  eg methane
      petrol vapour
      propane.

It may be more difficult to lift and carry things and movement generally is restricted and slowed down.

You may enter a confined space only when all the following conditions have been met:

- that work cannot be done without entering the confined space
- you are part of a trained team of sufficient number for the job
- you are working to and understand a written method statement, which preferably involves a permit-to-work control system
- all necessary atmosphere tests have been properly conducted and recorded, good ventilation is provided (or breathing apparatus is used) and continuous atmosphere tests will be undertaken
- you are equipped with adequate

    - overalls, gloves and footwear

    - breathing and head protection

    - safety harness, lighting and communications
- rescue arrangements and emergency procedures have been planned and you know them. Trained and suitably equipped person(s) must remain at the entrance of the confined space for the duration of the work.

9.1 Cranes and Hoists

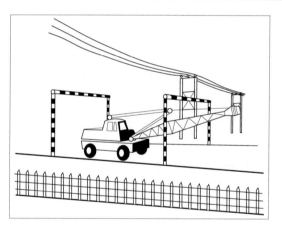

Fly jib

Outriggers are used to ensure crane stability

Travelling under power cables, use safety clearance goalposts

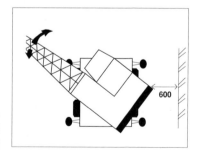

600

Provide at least 600mm clearance between cranes and any obstructions

All lifting operations need to be planned and managed.

Crane access:

- overall height, width and swept path of crane for delivery must be checked
- approach and working areas to be as level as possible
- ground surface to be capable of taking loads
- safe height for passage underneath power lines to be determined – by reading the marker plate underneath the wire, or by phoning the electricity company – and goal posts erected.

Crane siting:

- all cranes must be sited in a stable position
- maintain at least a 600mm clearance between cranes and obstructions to prevent anyone becoming trapped
- cranes must be sited **at least** jib length plus 6m away from overhead power lines, but distance varies with voltage. Mark the danger area with permanent stakes or flags and high visibility tape
- when the safe working distance cannot be maintained, contact the electricity company to investigate rerouting or disconnecting the electricity supply – this may not be simple and must be planned well in advance
- when there are several cranes on site they must be sited clear of each other to prevent possible fouling of the jibs and loads
- the working area must kept free of unnecessary obstructions and adequate lighting provided
- with outriggers fully extended the crane must be a safe distance away from excavations, slopes, underground services, soft ground, etc. Use grillages to distribute the load.

Excavators used for lifting

Excavators may only be used as cranes (ie the bucket supporting lifting gear) in accordance with HSE Guidance Note PM42.

9.3 Cranes and Hoists

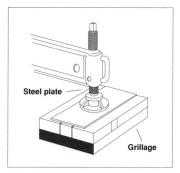

Steel plate

Grillage

Provide grillages to distribute the force from outriggers

Protect the load and the slings by providing packs

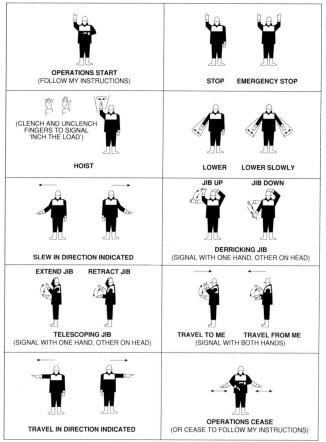

OPERATIONS START
(FOLLOW MY INSTRUCTIONS)

STOP   EMERGENCY STOP

(CLENCH AND UNCLENCH
FINGERS TO SIGNAL
'INCH THE LOAD')

HOIST

LOWER   LOWER SLOWLY

SLEW IN DIRECTION INDICATED

JIB UP   JIB DOWN

DERRICKING JIB
(SIGNAL WITH ONE HAND, OTHER ON HEAD)

EXTEND JIB   RETRACT JIB

TELESCOPING JIB
(SIGNAL WITH ONE HAND, OTHER ON HEAD)

TRAVEL TO ME   TRAVEL FROM ME
(SIGNAL WITH BOTH HANDS)

TRAVEL IN DIRECTION INDICATED

OPERATIONS CEASE
(OR CEASE TO FOLLOW MY INSTRUCTIONS)

Ensure that standard lifting signals are used and that only trained banksmen are employed

Crane operation.

All operations must have full regard for public safety. Never lift over areas used by the public.

Cranes must only be operated by trained and certificated drivers. Before starting lifting operations the driver must have documents recording the following prescribed information about the crane:

- weekly inspection
- thorough examination at a maximum interval of 14 months
- test and thorough examination within the last 4 years
- inspection every 6 months of chains, slings and lifting gear.

The crane must not be used if these documents are unavailable.

A trained banksman who will use only the standard signals should be present. It is essential that the crane driver knows who the banksman is. A third party should be appointed to plan and monitor the lifts.

All cranes with a lifting capacity above one tonne must have an automatic safe load indicator and the weight of all loads and the lifting radii should be determined in advance of lifting. A crane must not be allowed to operate with the safe load indicator bell sounding: if it does, check that the crane driver stops and inform your manager.

Use tail ropes to control unwieldy loads, eg formwork or bundles of scaffold tubes. Never use a single sling.

Each day the crane driver should:

- inspect the whole machine including ropes, tyres and tracks, lifting gear, including chains
- check that the automatic safe load indicator and load/radius indicators are working
- put the crane through all its movements to check brake and clutch operation.

9.5 Cranes and Hoists

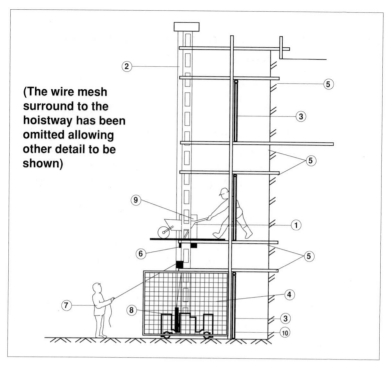

(The wire mesh surround to the hoistway has been omitted allowing other detail to be shown)

Sketch of a platform goods hoist

Safety rules for goods hoist operation:

1) No passengers to be carried
2) An over-run device must be fitted
3) 2m high gates at landings
4) The hoist must be enclosed appropriately
5) The hoist mast should be tied to the structure
6) A fall arrester device must be fitted
7) Operator must have clear view of whole hoist
8) Fail-safe operating control must be fitted
9) Safe working load must be displayed on the platform
10) Gates to be closed before the platform is moved.

Goods hoists.

There are 3 main hazards associated with goods hoists:

- falling down the hoistway
- being struck by the moving platform
- being hit by material falling from the platform.

Hoists must only be erected, extended and dismantled by competent, trained people. Hoist operators must be 18 or over and be trained to operate the hoist in question. The driver must be positioned so he can see the entire hoist.

Follow these rules for carrying materials on hoists:

- place loose materials (eg bricks) in a container or use a hoist with a cage; tall materials must be kept within the cage
- chock wheelbarrows or other mobile plant on the platform
- ensure that the safe working load is displayed on the platform and that it is not exceeded.

The following tests and records are required:

- the safe working load must be recorded in the prescribed manner
- every week the hoist must be inspected before use, and after alteration
- a thorough examination must be undertaken every 6 months.

These inspections and examinations must be recorded in the prescribed manner and documents must be available.

Never allow anyone to ride on a goods hoist. There are additional requirements for passenger hoists.

10.1 Demolition

Demolition work is particularly hazardous. It should only be carried out by competent and experienced demolition contractors.

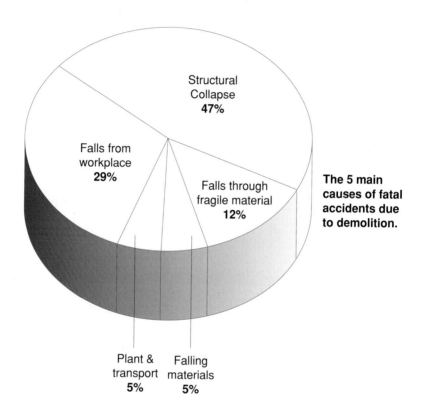

Structural Collapse **47%**

Falls from workplace **29%**

Falls through fragile material **12%**

The 5 main causes of fatal accidents due to demolition.

Plant & transport **5%**

Falling materials **5%**

If in doubt about the stability of a permanent or partly demolished structure, consult a structural engineer. Always check with your manager if you are concerned.

See also Chapters 8, 13 & 18

There are 3 main types of demolition:

- by hand
- by mechanical means
- by explosives.

Demolition by hand is the most hazardous and should be closely supervised.

Do not enter demolition sites without first getting permission from both the person in charge and your manager

The HSE produces a series of Guidance Notes on demolition – references GS29/1 to GS 29/4.

Key points include:

- safe distances from the structure must be established to eliminate the hazard of debris falling on workers or the public during explosive demolition of a factory chimney or multi-storey block
- the public and workers must be protected from falling materials by the use of properly constructed boarded fans. Fans are for protection only. Do not use them for access, stacking or storage of materials
- safe places of work must be provided, complete with guard rails and toeboards. When these cannot be provided, safety harnesses must be used
- temporary struts and guy ropes must be securely anchored and clearly marked or flagged.

 20 people die in demolition accidents in Britain every year.

10.3 Demolition

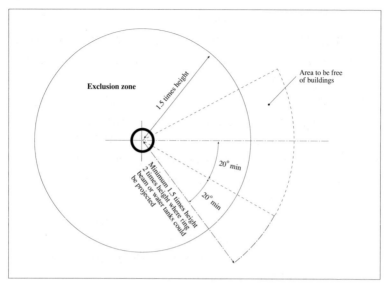

Demolition of a chimney or slender building. Where explosives are used, persons may be excluded from a larger zone

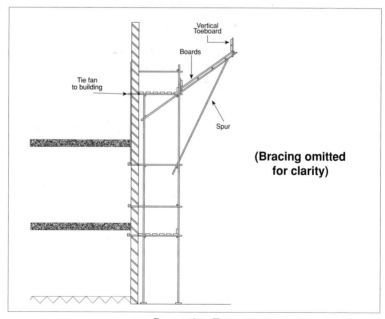

(Bracing omitted for clarity)

Protective Fan

Before demolition work starts:

- a written method statement must be prepared and agreed
- a competent person in charge of the operation must be nominated in writing
- a competent person must inspect the structure
- particular attention must be paid to insulation. If asbestos is found, it must be removed by a licensed contractor
- plans of the building structure must be obtained
- the utility companies must be contacted and all services disconnected or diverted
- existing floors, planned to be used as working platforms, must be suitable for that purpose
- windows must be removed and boarded over and glass stored safely prior to disposal
- all necessary shoring, lighting, signs, etc., must be planned and the work carried out at the correct time
- suitable PPE must be provided and used during operations.

During operations:

- adequate protection and safe access for the public and workers must be provided at all times, including protection from dust and noise hazards
- all the employees must be fit and trained for this work
- all machines must be suitable and placed in safe working positions
- overloading of existing floors (or any part of the structure) must not be permitted. Detection of any sign of weakness that might lead to structural instability must be referred to your manager immediately
- all plant machine cabs must be robust with shatterproof glass, mesh, etc.
- the method statement must be monitored and modified as necessary.

11.1 Electricity

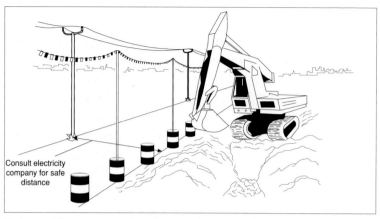

Safe working near overhead power lines requires a separation zone

There are many electrical hazards on a typical site, eg:

- 33kV overhead power lines
- 11kV buried or overhead cables
- 110V power tools
- energised installations in partly completed structures.

There is no safe voltage. Even a small shock can startle you and cause you to jump back causing a slip or fall. All electrical equipment should be considered dangerous.

Voltage	Sheathing Colour
25	Violet
50	White
110-130	Yellow
220-240	Blue
318-415	Red
500-750	Black

Guidance on voltages is given by the sheathing colour

 300 workers suffer major injuries from electric shock in Britain each year.

See also chapters 9 & 23

Overhead/underground cables

Consider the location of overhead and underground cables at the planning stage of a project. Overhead wires are not insulated. Electricity can jump air gaps and current can be induced in metal structures parallel to power lines.

The precise position of buried cables must be determined from utility plans and confirmed using cable locators and hand digging. Electric cables do not lie in straight lines, they snake about within a trench. These rules should be followed:

- consult the electricity company to arrange diversions, isolation, or permit-to-work arrangements
- erect clearly marked barriers to protect overhead power lines which remain live – provide 6m minimum clearance or as directed by the electricity company
- report any damage to the insulation of underground cables to the electricity company.

Electricity distribution and use on site:

- use portable electric tools powered by voltages of 110volts maximum, unless special prior arrangements have been agreed with your manager
- do not use home-made extension cables
- do not use multi-way adaptors or domestic 13 amp plugs
- do not make temporary repairs to electrical equipment
- check the condition of plugs, leads, power tools and controls
- use the correct leads and sockets for the voltage supplied
- check that fuses are of the correct rating
- ensure temporary electrical systems are properly installed and tested
- plan for regular inspection and maintenance of all distribution systems, power tools and electric appliances
- use residual current devices (earth leakage circuit breakers) at the point of supply for 240volts hand-held equipment.

12.1 Excavations

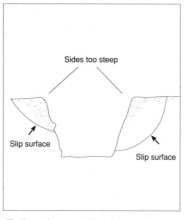

Failure by rotation in soft clays

Sides too steep

Slip surface

Slip surface

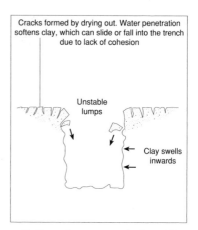

Cracks formed by drying out. Water penetration softens clay, which can slide or fall into the trench due to lack of cohesion

Unstable lumps

Clay swells inwards

Failure due to cracks in stiff clays

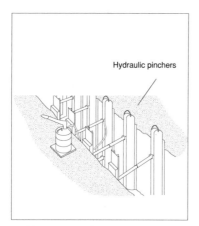

Hydraulic pinchers

Use hydraulically operated shoring devices instead of timber

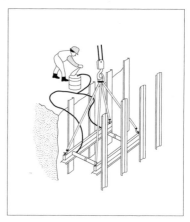

Work outside the trench whenever possible

No excavation can be considered safe, however shallow.

No ground can be considered totally stable: the ground may be inherently weak, laminated or have previously been disturbed.

Water may create instability in excavations. This can occur through:

- the action of rainwater
- changes in groundwater conditions
- erosion by water
- frost action
- drying out of soil.

It is essential that all excavations are made safe by:

- having sides battered to a safe angle of repose, or
- providing structural supports, eg trench sheets and struts, drag boxes, sheet piling or proprietary systems.

Trenches less than 1.2m deep may not require support if the ground is firm, provided that proper safety procedures exist and are always carried out. All trenches over 1.2m deep must have their sides adequately supported or be battered back to a safe slope.

Where ground and support arrangements allow, install the supports before excavation to final depth. The excavation and support installation should proceed by steps until final depth is reached. Adopt safe working practices, use proprietary systems which can be installed from outside the trench or work progressively forward from existing supports.

 8 people die in sudden excavations collapses in Britain every year.

12.3 Excavations

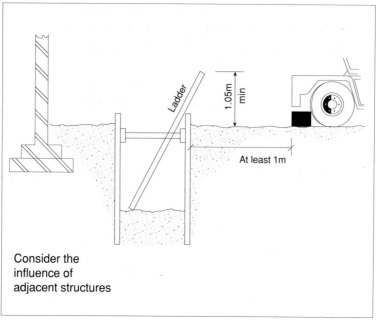

Consider the
influence of
adjacent structures

Protect the trench

Before work starts

All excavation work must be planned. Before digging
begins on site, check that arrangements have been made
to:

- locate underground services – check with all utility
  companies, look for indicator posts, use cable and pipe
  detectors

- establish ground conditions and design an adequate
  support system

- consider the interaction of proposed excavations and
  existing structures:
  - will the excavation de-stabilise existing structures?
  - do the existing structures have adequate foundations?
  - has the ground already been disturbed?

- provide edge protection for all excavations, use projecting trench sheets or other solid barriers where possible. If a person could fall more than 2m, suitable barriers must be provided
- ensure the person directly supervising the work is fully experienced and competent in the support of excavations
- obtain the necessary drawings or sketches
- brief and instruct operatives
- provide site security, particularly in relation to preventing children getting on to the site
- establish adequate working space for plant and for spoil heaps (spoil heaps and materials should not be less than 1m from the edge of the excavation)
- construct bridges or gangways as required
- provide sufficient ladders secured against movement
- assess need for lighting
- issue appropriate protective clothing and equipment.

12.5 Excavations

During the work

The excavation and its supports must be inspected by a competent person at the start of each shift, to address the following questions:

- is access to and from the work face sufficient and secure?

- are all working faces secure, wedges tight and support material free from damage?

- is there any sign of movement or deflection in the support system?

- is the soil condition as predicted? If not, what action should be taken?

- are spoil heaps an adequate distance back from the trench edge?

- are pipes, bricks and other materials, plant etc., well clear of the edge so that there is no risk of them falling into the trench or of vibration causing danger to the support?

- is the method statement being properly followed in installing the support? (This is particularly important in relation to the spacing of walings and struts)

- are regular tests for gases or fumes being carried out? Is ventilation required?

- have risks of flooding been properly assessed?

- where pumping is necessary, is a proper watch being kept to make sure that fine material is not being drawn out from behind the support system?

- is resuscitation equipment available and a nominated person trained to use it?

- have all persons been instructed in excavation procedure and the correct rescue procedure to follow if someone is overcome by gases or fumes in the trench?

- are operatives wearing safety helmets? Is any other protective equipment needed?

- is the work adequately protected and marked during the day? Is it fenced, or covered, and lit at night? Are watchmen needed?

- do gangways or bridges comply with the requirements of the Construction (Working Places) Regulations in relation to width, guardrails and toeboards. Have access bridges for plant and vehicles crossing the excavation been designed by competent persons?

- where backfilling is required, are vehicle stop blocks in position?

- is there an agreed system of support withdrawal and have those carrying it out been properly instructed?

An additional weekly inspection must also be made and recorded.

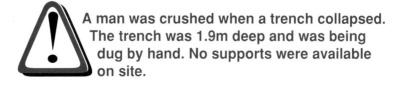

A man was crushed when a trench collapsed. The trench was 1.9m deep and was being dug by hand. No supports were available on site.

13.1 Falling

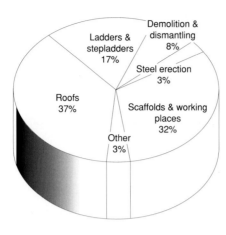

The working situations from which construction workers fall to their deaths

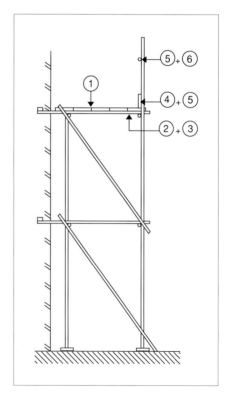

Preventing falls from an independent tied scaffold

(See checklist opposite)

See also
Chapter 20

Scaffolds should be designed, erected, altered or dismantled only under the direction of a competent person and by competent and experienced workers. Scaffolds should be inspected weekly by a competent person and the inspection recorded.

Does your scaffold adequately meet the requirements to reduce the risks of falling?
Check these points as a guide for traditional scaffolds:

1. platform 3-5 boards wide, depending on use

2. each scaffold board on a working platform to have at least three supports – supports not more than 1.5m apart

3. scaffold boards either tied down or overhanging each end support by at least 50mm but not more than 4 times the thickness of the board

4. guardrails and toeboards along the outside edge and at the ends of any working platform from which people or materials could fall more than 2m. Use guardrails and toe boards at inside edge where gap exceeds 300mm

5. toeboards at least 150mm high with no more than 750mm between the top of the toeboard and the guardrail

6. guardrail 910-1150mm above the platform.

 In a recent 5 year period there were 383 constructions deaths by falling.

13.3 Falling – from Roofs

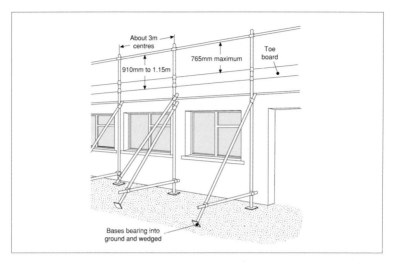

Edge protection on a flat roof using tube and fitting scaffolding

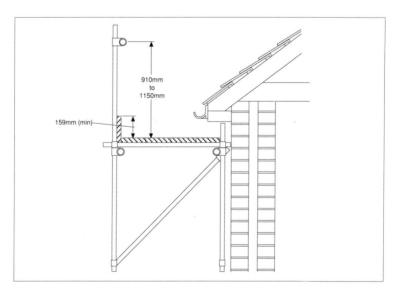

Edge protection on a sloping roof using tube and fitting scaffolding

Falling – from Roofs 13.4

The main hazards include:

- falls from flat or sloping roofs
- falls through fragile roofs
- falls from ladders or scaffolds.

To minimise the risks, follow these rules:

- be aware of the precautions to be followed when working at heights
- display prominent permanent warning notices at the approach to any fragile roof
- never walk on fragile materials such as asbestos cement or glass. Beware – they may have been painted over or covered with insulation
- always use a planned means of access such as crawling boards or a proprietary system
- on a flat roof make sure that the edge is protected by a parapet and/or guardrails and that the roof is strong enough to support you
- where someone could fall over the edge of the roof, guardrails and toeboards must be installed or anchorage points for safety harnesses provided. Make sure that safety harnesses are worn
- prevent items falling onto people below – use brick guards, toeboards and warning notices
- keep off roofs in bad weather, eg high winds (especially if carrying sheet materials) or where there may be other hazards such as fumes from flue outlets or heavy frost.

When working above ground level there is no safe height.

13.5 Falling – from Ladders

An engineer fell 4m while descending a ladder. He was advising on the renovation of a balcony. A fully boarded out scaffold had been erected and access was obtained using a ladder which was not secured but was footed by an assistant. Unfortunately, when the engineer came to descend he did not check that the assistant still had the ladder footed securely. The assistant was caught unawares, the base slipped and the engineer fell onto the pavement.

Always follow these rules:

- secure ladders against slipping when possible by tying at the top. A second person standing at the foot to prevent slipping is effective only with ladders less than about 5m long. For longer ladders use stakes etc.

- ladders should extend at least 1m above the landing place or the highest rung in use, unless an alternative hand hold is available

- arrange ways of carrying tools and materials up and down so that both hands are free to grip the ladder

- use a ladder stay or similar device to avoid placing ladders against a fragile support, eg plastic gutters

- never place ladders where there is danger from moving vehicles, overhead cranes or electricity lines

- ensure that ladders have level and firm footings - never use unsteady bases such as oil drums, boxes or planks

- do not support ladders on their rungs

- extending ladders should have an overlap of at least three rungs

- set ladders at a slope of four to one

- check ladders regularly for defects – never use damaged or 'home-made' ladders. Take damaged ladders out of use.

A demolition worker tripped over a pneumatic hose and fell 4.6m while working at an open edge on a demolition site.

A foreman fell 3.7m from the edge of a floor. The guard rail had been removed so that he could use a power float. After the accident an alternative method of fixing the guard was devised so that the float could be used effectively.

A bricklayer tripped over a pile of asbestos sheets lying on his working platform. He fell 3.3m head first over the edge to his death. Toe-boards and guard rails had been removed and not reinstated.

Remember:

- keep all working places and access routes tidy and free of tripping hazards
- provide guardrails between 910 and 1150mm high and toe boards at least 150mm high
- provide adequate lighting
- clearly sign incomplete or dangerous scaffolds and working platforms and prevent access
- devise, implement, monitor and review safe systems of work whenever falling is a hazard
- openings in floors should be provided with a secure cover and marked appropriately.

 Falling is the greatest single cause of death on construction sites.

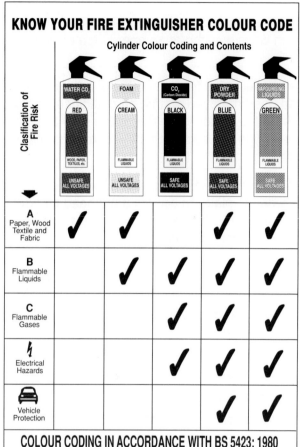

KNOW YOUR FIRE EXTINGUISHER COLOUR CODE

Cylinder Colour Coding and Contents

Clasification of Fire Risk	WATER CO_2 RED WOOD, PAPER, TEXTILES, etc. UNSAFE ALL VOLTAGES	FOAM CREAM FLAMMABLE LIQUIDS UNSAFE ALL VOLTAGES	CO_2 (Carbon Dioxide) BLACK FLAMMABLE LIQUIDS SAFE ALL VOLTAGES	DRY POWDER BLUE FLAMMABLE LIQUIDS SAFE ALL VOLTAGES	VAPOURISING LIQUIDS GREEN FLAMMABLE LIQUIDS SAFE ALL VOLTAGES
A Paper, Wood Textile and Fabric	✓	✓		✓	✓
B Flammable Liquids		✓	✓	✓	✓
C Flammable Gases			✓	✓	✓
Electrical Hazards			✓	✓	✓
Vehicle Protection				✓	✓

COLOUR CODING IN ACCORDANCE WITH BS 5423:1980 - SPECIFICATION FOR PORTABLE FIRE EXTINGUISHERS

The symbol shows the three conditions for fire – remove any one and the fire will stop

Approximately 700 people suffer serious burns on British construction sites each year.

> **See also chapters 5 & 7**

Fire prevention is much better than fire fighting:

- flammable waste must be stored tidily on site awaiting disposal
- burning of rubbish on site must be controlled
- flammable materials must be stored away from hazardous processes, eg welding, fabrication areas
- all flammable material stores must have warning signs
- petrol driven plant must be switched off before refuelling and a funnel used to avoid splashes
- smoking must be prohibited within 6m of flammable liquid and gas cylinders, NO SMOKING signs prominently displayed and good ventilation provided
- heating and cooking appliances must be properly installed
- many fires are caused by carelessness in drying wet clothes over fires/heaters.

Hot work, eg burning and welding, requires special consideration:

- remove combustible material to beyond the area of sparks and spatter or provide flameproof protection
- do not use tarpaulins as protection against sparks
- the work site must be checked after the hot work is completed, as fires can smoulder for hours.

Adequate fire extinguishers must be provided on all sites. Site personnel must know:

- the correct types of extinguisher and their location, their colour code and limitations of use
- how to use the extinguishers provided.

Each site must have a fire emergency plan. All persons must know what that plan is and the part they play in it.

15.1 Frame Erection

Mobile access plant should be used whenever possible

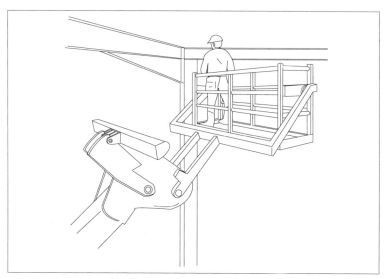

Telescopic hydraulic work platform in use for steel erection

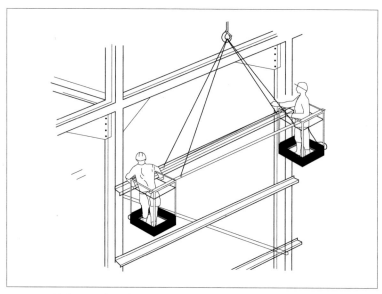

Using a sheeting rail cradle to provide safe access

See also
Chapters 13 & 20

There are 4 main hazards associated with frame erection:

- falling
- being struck by falling tools or materials
- collapse of the partly erected structure
- adverse weather conditions.

Consideration of safety during frame erection should start at the design stage and be carried through by means of a written method statement for the site work.

Design stage – consideration should include:

- stability during all stages of erection of the structure
- the effect of the erection sequence on stability
- assessment of loading at all stages of construction, including temporary loads due to erection
- safe means of connecting components including safe access and working places – consider using remote handling where possible
- safe handling, lifting and transportation
- recognition of the practical problems of the steel erector, eg access to make connections.

For the erection of very heavy or complex members a representative from the design team may need to be present to ensure that no confusion or misunderstanding of the safe erection procedure occurs.

> **Keep out of the area of frame erection unless it is absolutely necessary to be there. Obtain the erection supervisor's permission before you enter the area.**

15.3 Frame Erection

Erection stage – the method statement should include:

- scheme management and co-ordination, responsibilities and authority of personnel at all levels and the provision and maintenance of effective communication

- erection sequence including use of remote handling

- methods of ensuring stability at all times (including overnight) of individual components (including columns) and sub-assemblies, as well as partially erected structures

- a detailed method of erecting the structure and an erection scheme devised to ensure that lifting, initial connecting, unslinging, and final connecting are carried out safely

- procedures for work in the event of adverse weather conditions, eg high winds

- measures to prevent falls from height such as safe access and safe places of work. These may include special platforms and walkways, mobile towers, mobile access plant, slung, suspended or other scaffolds, secured ladders, safety harness, safety nets and supervision to ensure that all equipment is properly used

- provision of barriers such as screens, fans and nets for protection from falls of material and tools

- provision of suitable plant (including cranes) and tools and equipment of sufficient strength, capability and quantity

- contingency back-up in the event of breakdown of essential plant and equipment

- delivery, stacking, movement on site and on-site fabrication or pre-assembly

- details of site features, layout and siting of offices and stores, with notes on how these may affect proposed erection procedures.

16.1 Manual Handling

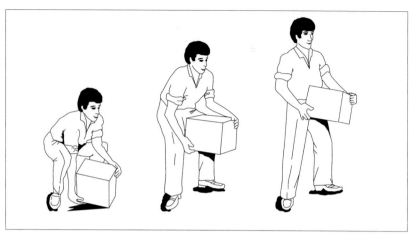

Bend your knees, not your back

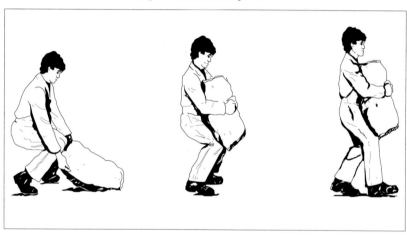

**Keep your back straight, lift with your legs
and look where you are going**

 Back injuries are the greatest single cause
of sick leave.

See also
Chapter 9

Size up the job:
- are the floors sloping, slippery or greasy?
- are there obstructions or stairs?
- if the object is too heavy to lift, get help
- know where the object is to be put down.

Stand firmly:
- stand close to the load
- place your feet about 0.5m apart
- place one foot in front of the other in the direction of movement.

Bend your knees:
- keep your back straight
- keep your chin well in.

Get a firm grip:
- use the whole of your fingers – not just the finger tips
- keep the load close to your body
- grip boxes diagonally.

Lift with your legs:
- lift by straightening your legs
- keep your back straight
- use the impetus of the lift and start moving off in the required direction.

Putting things down:
- keep your back straight
- bend your knees
- don't trap your fingers
- put the load down askew and slide it into place.

> **Always use mechanical aids for lifting heavy and awkward objects. Get help when necessary.**

17.1 Noise

Sound pressure in decibels	Situation	Sound pressure in pascals
	- Peak action level, immediate irreversible damage	200
		100
140	- Jet at 30m	
130	- Threshold of pain	
	- Pneumatic breaker (unsilenced) at 1m	
120	- Pneumatic digger	10
	- 600 HP scraper at 2m (pass by)	
110	- Rock drill	
	- Diesel hammer driving sheet steel at 10m	
100	- Scabbling	1
	- 7 HP road roller on concrete at 10m	
95	- Concrete pouring	
90	- Second action level	
	- Drilling/grinding concrete	0.1
85	- First action level	
80	- Scaffold dismantling at 10m	
	- 8 HP diesel hoist at 10m	
70		
	- 5 HP power float at 7m	0.01
60		
	- Typical office	
50		
	- Living room	

Typical Sound Intensities

Sound pressure is measured in pascals or decibels (dB). The decibel scale is logarithmic and it doubles with every increase of 3dB, ie 78dB is twice as loud as 75dB and 81dB is 4 times as loud.

The effect of noise on the hearing is cumulative. Noise exposure is normalised to an 8 hour working day over a 40 year working life.

Whenever possible, limit noise at source.

Exposure to high levels of noise over extended periods will damage your hearing. Noise-induced hearing loss is irreversible.

See also
Chapter 3

Loud noises can cause:

- permanent damage to hearing
- your hearing to become less sensitive
- permanent ringing in the ears
- breakdown of safe communication.

If, with normal hearing, you have difficulty conducting a normal conversation at 1m, the noise level is about 90dB; difficulty at 2m means the noise level is about 85dB. Move away!

The Noise At Work Regulations require employers:

- to assess noise levels
- at the **First Action Level of 85dB** to provide employees with information about the risks to hearing and provide hearing protection on request
- at the **Second Action Level of 90dB** to control noise exposure by:
  - limiting the noise at source, as the first step
  - requiring hearing protection to be worn
  - limiting the time people are exposed to noise
- at the **Peak Action Level of 200 pascals** to control noise exposure. The Peak Action Level is relevant to single loud noises and can cause instantaneous hearing damage eg use of cartridge tools in an enclosed space.

Using environmental legislation, Local Authorities have the power to serve notices which specify noise levels, limit working hours for noisy operations, or ban certain types of machines if complaints are received. If you are served with such a notice CONTACT YOUR MANAGER IMMEDIATELY.

> **When you are in a hearing protection area, wear your ear defenders all the time; removing ear defenders for only half an hour in 8 hours reduces the overall protection afforded by 40%.**

18.1 Pressure Testing

General

All pressure tests must be conducted in accordance with a written method statement.

Before pressure testing begins, the following must be checked for damage, correct alignment, jointing integrity and compatibility:
- pipes
- valves
- fittings and flange connections
- pipeline restraints.

Pressure testing must not be carried out until all these are correct.

Pipes and fittings should be checked to ensure that they are designed to pass the pressure test plus allowable overload.

Whenever practicable, hydraulic pressure testing should be used. Air is 20,000 times more compressible than water and the sudden release of a large volume of compressed air is in effect an explosion. Use pneumatic testing only when hydraulic testing is unacceptable.

At the pressure ranges normally encountered, the amount of energy stored in compressed air or gas is 200 times that contained in water at the same pressure and volume.

All pressure testing, if not carefully controlled, can be dangerous. Sudden release of uncontrolled pressure acts like an explosion and can kill and maim. Always read the contract specification and manufacturers' instructions to determine the maximum pressure during testing. Do not exceed it.

Hydraulic testing:

- people working in the area should be warned before hydraulic tests begin

- it should be established before a test commences that all anchorages are in position, that concrete anchorages are adequately designed for test pressure and have developed the required strength and that where the pipes are laid to produce large radius curves, the backfill between the pipe body and the trench side is well compacted

- air valves or suitable tappings should be located at appropriate high points of the main to allow the air to escape while the pipe is being filled. If the pipeline is on a level grade, it may be necessary to bleed air off at several points to ensure complete evacuation. After the air has been evacuated all vent holes must be plugged

- where the joints of buried pipelines are to be left uncovered until testing has been completed, sufficient backfill material should be placed over the body of each pipe to prevent movement

- each section to be tested should be properly sealed off with special stop ends designed for the safe introduction and disposal of the test water and release of air

- stop ends should be secured by adequate temporary anchors. The thrust on the stop ends should be calculated and temporary anchors designed accordingly

- the section under test should be filled with clean water, taking care that all air is displaced. Where the pipeline will be used for carrying potable water, the water used for testing should be clean and disinfected.

Never use oxygen, propane, acetylene or any flammable gas to pressure test pipelines.

19.1 Public Safety and Site Security

Major causes of fatalities to the public, arising from construction work and lapses of site security are:

- being struck by falling objects
- falling from height
- being struck by moving plant or equipment
- falling into holes and drowning or being crushed (particularly children)
- hazards present in partially completed work. Many injuries are caused by tripping over unexpected obstacles.

Children:

- construction sites are a magnet to children
- wherever possible, arrange for a company safety officer to visit local schools to warn of construction site dangers
- consult HSE Guidance Note GS7, "Accidents to Children On Construction Sites", for further precautions to be taken.

Storms

When high winds are forecast and before every site shutdown (eg Christmas) pay particular attention to:

- scaffolding, ie check ties, sheeting, bracing, boards and all connections and foundations
- stability and security of boundary fences
- storage including sheet materials and waste materials, eg empty chemical containers
- stability of lighting towers, cranes, hoardings and all temporary works.

> ⚠ Over a recent 5 year period, 63 members of the public were killed and 784 seriously injured by construction activities. More than 30% were children.

See also,
Chapters 9, 17 & 26

General

All employers and employees have a general duty under Section 3 of the Health and Safety at Work etc. Act to take reasonably practicable measures to minimise risks to the general public. These include:

- secure site fences wherever practicable. Warning signs displayed and access gates kept locked outside working hours

- safety zones to separate the public from construction works. This is particularly important for roadworks and multi-storey works in city centres. In such cases consultation with the Highway Authority must take place

- sites which cannot be fenced off should have high visibility barriers, warning signs and adequate lighting and security staff as appropriate

- material must never be thrown or dropped from a height in an uncontrolled way

- securely support and guard all excavation to limit public access – provide lighting and secure fencing for these areas

- material deliveries and site activities (eg scaffold tube hoisting) to be organised to avoid lifting operations over roads and pavements which are open to the public. If such lifting is unavoidable, arrange diversions and/or closures

- mobile plant and equipment is to be immobilised when it is not in use. Small plant, bottled gases and chemicals are to be securely stored in their approved places

- construction operation in public areas must cause minimum disruption to pedestrians and road users.

 One member of the public is killed by construction activities each month on average.

20.1 Scaffolding – Mobile

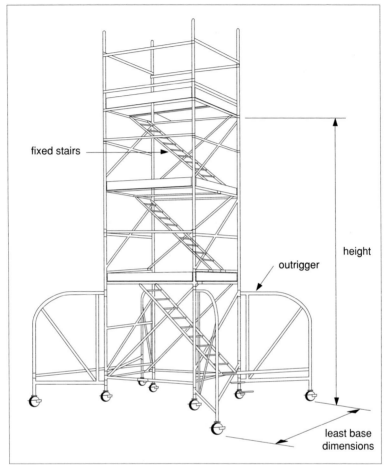

A typical tower scaffold.

There are two main hazards associated with both mobile and fixed scaffolding:

- people and/or materials falling from the scaffold
- overturning or collapse of the scaffold.

Chapter 13 deals with falling. This chapter deals with precautions against scaffold collapse or overturning.

> See also
> Chapters 13 & 24

Tower scaffolds:

- the scaffold is to be erected in accordance with the manufacturer's instructions and the safe working load restrictions are to be observed
- the tower must rest on a firm base on level ground. Use the outriggers and ensure the castors are locked before the tower is used
- the ratio of height to least base dimension should not exceed 3:1 for outside work, or 3.5:1 for inside work, unless tied
- never use a ladder on or against the top platform of a tower scaffold. Use only internal ladders/stairs for access to the working platform – never use the scaffold framework as a ladder unless it is purpose-designed
- tower scaffolds must not be used outside during winds of force 4 or greater unless securely tied
- the tower is to be securely tied to the structure whenever it is to be used for grit blasting, heavy drilling, or it is to be sheeted out
- overhead power lines and obstructions must be considered when constructing, using or moving the tower
- the tower must never be moved with people or materials on the working platform
- once the move is completed the outriggers must be re-engaged and the castors locked
- must not be used unless they have been inspected by a competent person within the previous 7 days.

 One person dies in a scaffolding accident every fortnight on average on a British construction site.

20.3 Scaffolding – Fixed

This section applies to conventional tube and fitting scaffolds.

Support the standards on a secure base

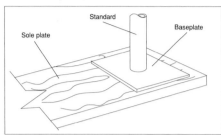

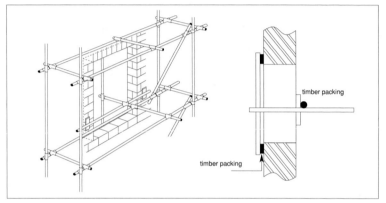

A through tie

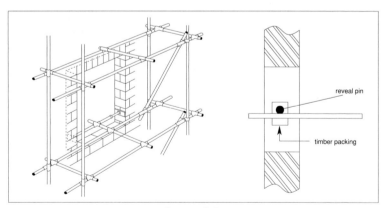

A reveal tie

> **Removal, renewal or alteration of ties should only be carried out by a competent and authorised scaffolder.**

General access scaffold:

- for scaffolding to be safe, it must be stable and designed to take the anticipated load. This depends on a properly established base, a suitable height in relation to its mean base dimension or being tied to a permanent structure to prevent movement
- scaffolds must be erected in accordance with BS 5973 and the Construction (Working Places) Regulations 1966.

Base:

- level wooden sole plate (positioned from outside to inside standard) surmounted by steel base plate with central spigot to prevent displacement of the standard
- daily check to ensure no undermining.

Standards (upright tubes)

Must be vertical with staggered joints made by internal expanded fittings.

Ledgers (running longitudinally parallel to the structure):

- joined by externally placed clamp (sleeve coupler) staggered to ensure joints do not fall in same bay
- ledger secured to standards with right-angle couplers (load bearing).

Transoms (tubes placed on ledger at right angles to the structure):

- these complete the square of scaffolding and are used as supports for boards
- there must be a transom provided adjacent to every standard joined with right angle load-bearing couplers
- intermediate transoms provided to support boards may be joined with wrap-over fittings (non load-bearing).

Ledger brace:

- a tube running diagonally from upper rear to front lower ledger in alternate bays of scaffolding
- load-bearing couplers must be used
- may run from standard to standard (use load bearing swivel coupler)
- may all run in same direction or in reverse of each other (dog-leg bracing).

Longitudinal facade or face brace

Fitted from base to top of scaffold at a diagonal across the face to prevent bowing of the face or sway movement.

Ties

Ties must be provided. Only 50% of ties in a scaffold may be reveal ties.

- through tie – a tie assembly through a window or opening in a wall
- reveal tie – tube placed into window reveal with screw fitting
- box tie – made by encompassing column or outer part of permanent structure
- drilled anchorages – female part fitted to suitably sound part of the structure, male part attached to scaffold to tie to the building
- where ties do not prevent inward movement this must be done by abutting the transoms to the face of the building
- ties must not be fitted to external decorative fittings, eg down pipes or balustrades.

Working platforms

Must be even and fully boarded – width depends on usage of scaffold.

Toeboards and guard rails

Required on all working platforms, access ways, stairways and landings, where a fall of more than 2 metres is possible.

Access to working platforms

Access normally by ladders or stairways. Ladder must be tied and at an angle of 4:1.

Loading

Loading should be vertically above the standards where possible or at specially strengthened loading bays.

NOTE: The wall thickness of scaffold tubes can vary, eg UK tube is thicker than European tube, and therefore load bearing capacities can vary. Tubes of different thicknesses or of different metals (ie steel and alloy) should not be mixed in a designed structure.

Remember

No scaffold - fixed or mobile - should be used unless it has been inspected by a competent person:

- **within the previous 7 days**
- **after exposure to adverse weather conditions which may have affected its strength or stability**
- **after any substantial modification or alteration.**

All inspections must record the prescribed information.

21.1 Site Investigation

Initial survey

Before going to site consider the hazards you may encounter. These can include:

- surveying on live roads
- contaminated land
- dilapidated buildings
- confined spaces
- old cellars, walls or shafts
- unstable ground or pits
- live services
- asbestos.

Consider which hazards you may meet, and how they could affect you – THEN PLAN SAFE SYSTEMS OF WORK.

Site investigation

Drilling and digging trial pits will expose the ground investigation team to hazards including:

- contaminated land – COSHH assessments required
- collapse of ground
- methane (or other gas) pockets – the agreed safe system of work must include gas detection, testing and emergency procedures
- underground services.

The following general rules apply to site investigation:

- there should be a minimum of 2 drilling crew per rig
- never enter an unsupported trial pit
- appropriate lighting, barriers and warning signs must be provided at the end of each working day
- staff must wash their hands before eating or drinking
- eating, drinking and smoking should only be allowed in designated clean areas, eg a site mess cabin
- adequate storage must be provided for dirty clothing and PPE.

Existing services include:

- overhead and underground electric and telephone cables
- water
- gas
- chemical pipelines
- cable TV
- sewerage.

Standard colour codes are gradually being adopted for services. Ask your manager.

All services present hazards – the first essential move towards avoiding danger from overhead or underground services to is to contact the local offices of the relevant company – British Telecom, British Gas, electricity, water and cable companies and highway authorities, and obtain as much information as possible about the location of cables, lines and pipes. Thereafter, it is important to maintain close liaison with the companies as long as the work is in progress.

Erect goalposts and barriers to protect overhead services and use cable locators to pinpoint the location of underground services.

After use of locators (by trained personnel), trial holes should be carefully dug, using hand tools, to confirm the position of buried services.

Once underground services have been located it is important to identify them correctly. Consult the service companies for confirmation and to record their location, type and depth permanently.

The use of hand-held power tools and mechanical excavators too close to underground services is a major cause of accidents.

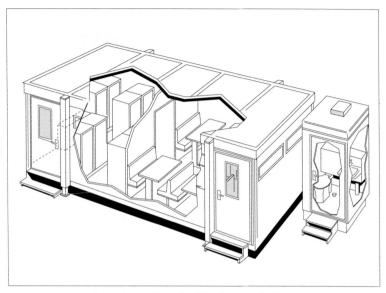

A basic welfare facility for small sites

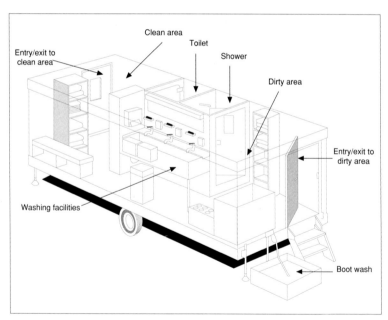

Clean area

Toilet

Entry/exit to
clean area

Shower

Dirty area

Entry/exit to
dirty area

Washing facilities

Boot wash

A good standard of hygiene facility for contaminated sites

See also
Chapters 4, 19 & 30

Site organisation

Health, safety and welfare standards are reinforced by the early provision of:

- adequate canteen, hygiene and first aid facilities and toilets
- a secure perimeter fencing to the site
- clearly defined site access
- vehicle washing facilities
- all necessary PPE and adequate storage space for PPE
- clearly defined storage, office and working areas
- emergency procedures and statutory notices posted in highly visible places
- a mobile phone until fixed phones are installed.

Notify the emergency services of site location, activities and access.

Major sites should have a fully equipped first-aid room but every site must have:

- soap, towels and clean hot water for washing
- at least one first-aid box
- small portable first-aid kits for people who do not have easy access to the first-aid box.

First-aid boxes should have a list of contents inside the lid.

Your company must provide an adequate number of fully trained first-aiders or appointed persons who must be readily identifiable.

All employees should receive site induction training including details of the site layout, site rules and emergency procedures. Visitors should always be accompanied. Do not enter a site alone without first informing others.

23.1 Small Plant and Equipment

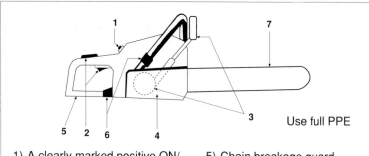

1) A clearly marked positive ON/OFF switch
2) Safety (dead hand) throttle
3) Front hand guard/chain brake
4) Chain catcher

5) Chain breakage guard
6) Anti-vibration handles
7) Safety chain to reduce risk of kick back

Use full PPE

Chain Saw Guards

Small plant must be used with the correct PPE

20% of all construction fatalities – that is 30 deaths every year – occur as a result of accidents with mobile plant and equipment.

See also Chapter 3

All small plant and equipment is potentially dangerous.
Small plant and equipment frequently involved in accidents
includes:

- saws
- abrasive wheels
- cartridge-operated fixing tools
- compressed air tools.

Cutting, drilling, grinding, punching or sawing with small
plant is dangerous.

Small plant and equipment:

- affects others working nearby
- must be used only by trained and authorised personnel
- must be kept clean and well maintained
- must have all guards fitted and effective
- can create noise and dust
- requires the wearing of appropriate PPE
- should be kept in locked stores when not in use. Stores
  must be clean, dry, well lit and well ventilated, and have
  an issue/recovery control system
- fuels should be kept and transported in suitable, properly
  labelled containers.

Maintenance:

All plant and equipment requires regular maintenance.
Daily checks are part of these procedures and are to be
monitored.

Examples of daily checks on chain saws:

- stop switch – works
- guide bar and sprockets – not broken
- chain brake – works
- lubrication system – full.

24.1 Temporary Works

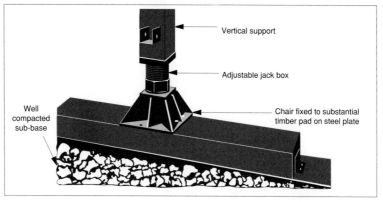

A good foundation detail for a load bearing base

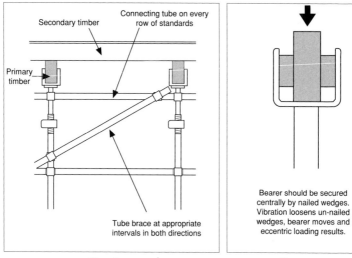

Bracing

Bearers

A temporary works coordinator should be appointed prior to work starting. He will be responsible for checking and signing for each stage of the works.

Temporary works include:

- falsework and formwork
- cofferdams and their bracing systems
- temporary supports to unstable structures

- temporary bridging
- scaffolding
- support to excavations
- temporary electrical supplies.

Design:

- all temporary works must be designed by qualified, experienced people
- calculations, drawings and sketches to explain and illustrate the temporary works design must be produced
- an independent design check should be carried out also considering any effects on the permanent works.

Method statement

A written method statement for construction and use of the temporary works is essential. It must include:

- the name of the person in charge
- detail of the design and loading limitations
- construction details and erection sequence
- a detailed loading sequence
- a specification for plant, materials and methods to be used
- details of supervision, inspection and checks to be made
- design tolerances, eg deflection/elongation
- striking times and sequence
- dismantling sequence.

The method statement must be checked and signed.

> **There must be no unauthorised departure from temporary works design or method statements. Authority must only be given in writing by temporary works designer (coordinator).**

25.1 Vehicles and Site Transport

Never ride on mobile plant

Avoid working close to plant and equipment whenever possible

 Every year many people are killed or injured on site by reversing vehicles.

See also Chapters 4 & 11

Large mobile plant:

- must use planned site entry and exit points only and obey appropriate traffic control procedures
- should be operated only by trained, authorised and licensed drivers aged 18 years or older
- must comply fully with the Road Traffic Act when it travels on public roads
- should have an instruction book which details the driver's daily checks and routine maintenance
- should have amber rotating lights
- reversing areas should be controlled by a banksman and non-essential personnel excluded
- when tipping into or running alongside excavations must be provided with stop blocks and scotches
- must not be overloaded
- carry only well secured loads
- must observe site speed limits – these must be clearly signed
- must be immobilised when not in use
- should be parked on level ground, in neutral with the parking brake applied
- may deposit mud and debris on public roads. Appropriate road cleaning arrangements must be provided
- has limitations on the gradients and cross-slopes on which it can safely operate. These must be observed.

All plant and powered equipment must be operated only by trained people who are authorised to use it.

26.1 Working on Live Roads

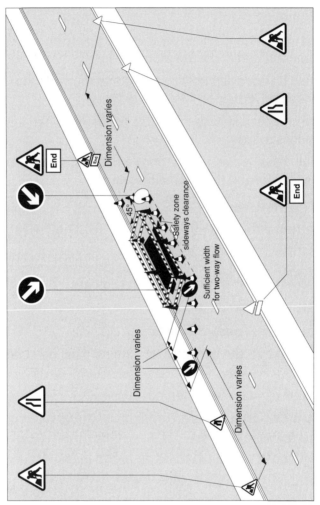

Traffic control on a single carriageway, using priority signs

Traffic safety measures at roadworks are covered by Chapter 8, Volumes 1 and 2 of the "Traffic Signs Manual" prepared by the DTp and published by HMSO. A simpler version "Safer Road Works Ahead" – a booklet for road workers and supervisors is also available.

See also
Chapter 25

Planning stage:

- local authorities and police must be consulted – and their requirements regarding the timing of the works implemented
- consult "Traffic Signs Manual" for details of signing requirements and size of safety zones
- decide how many of the following will be required:
  - traffic signs
  - cones
  - barriers
  - road lamps
  - information boards
  - site lighting.
- will traffic control systems be required, eg temporary traffic lights or Stop/Go boards?
- access must be planned to eliminate dangerous movements of site traffic (eg reversing of vehicles) and personnel (eg crossing dual carriageways)
- will the work be completed in daylight hours? If not, lighting must be provided
- all workers must wear high-visibility clothing
- vehicles should be equipped with amber flashing beacons.

On site:

- define the working area in the live road/footway
- define the working space – this includes the areas for storage of tools and equipment and space to move around the job
- provide a safety zone – this is an area to separate the work from the traffic – it must be kept clear of all work, materials storage and people and must be clear of the working radius of all plant
- work must be undertaken by certificated supervisors (from July 1994) and certificated operatives (from July 1997)
- minimum lane sizes and provision of adequate safety zones may result in the need for road closures. In that case the work will need to be replanned from scratch.

27.1 Working over Water

Combined harness and life jacket

Rescue line

Where there is a risk of people falling into water, provision must be made for:

- signs to warn of deep water
- edge protection, including guard rails and toe boards
- suitable rescue equipment and training in its use
- keeping platforms and ladders clean and clear of debris, slime and tripping hazards
- safety nets to limit falls to a maximum of 6m where standard working platforms cannot be provided
- safety lines and harnesses to be used in conjunction with temporary ladder access over water.

The wearing of some types of protective clothing can increase the risk of drowning. Non-slip work boots are preferable to wellington boots and chin straps should not be worn on safety helmets.

 75% of drownings occur in relatively quiet waters like ponds, reservoirs and rivers.

Rescue equipment:

- lifebuoys with rescue lines should be provided at intervals along the site and positioned conveniently for use in an emergency. Grab lines should be attached at intervals to structures or floating plant
- personnel must wear life jackets, or buoyancy aid equipped with a whistle and (during darkness) lights
- before the start of each shift all rescue equipment must be checked by a competent person to ensure it is present and in good condition
- enough personnel should be present who are trained in the use of rescue equipment
- resuscitation equipment should be provided at all first-aid points.

Rescue boats:

- on tidal water or fast flowing rivers, a power-driven boat should be provided and properly equipped, including lifebuoy with buoyant rope. In certain circumstances, eg some canals and inland waterways, a rowing boat may be sufficient
- where rescue boats are required during the hours of darkness, swivelling searchlights should be fitted
- rescue boats must be manned continuously during the period that any persons are working over water and when on standby
- rescue boats must be manned by experienced boatmen who are also trained first-aiders
- rescue boats should not be used for other purposes.

28.1 Working Alone

Never work alone in the following situations:

- in confined spaces
- over or near water
- on live electrical equipment.

If possible avoid working alone in the following situations:

- on live roads
- in derelict buildings
- on roofs
- near demolition work.

Although there is no general legal prohibition on working alone, the hazards that all workers face are increased when there is no one else to give a warning. Also because there is no-one else to help in the event of an accident, the risk of serious injury becomes more likely from:

- tripping, slipping and falling
- becoming trapped or crushed
- electrocution
- asphyxiation.

Plan your work:

- evaluate the work to be done – are the workplace and access to it safe? Is more than one person required?
- will any lifting be necessary – can one person do this safely?

Think carefully before you work alone.

See also
Chapter 30

Communicate:

- leave details of your movements at a designated place - state where you are going, when you will be there, when you expect to finish and where you will go next
- report in by phone or radio at regular pre-set intervals
- always report in when you leave a site – this is particularly important when you are not returning to your office or normal site base
- if there are other activities in the area make sure your presence is known to those in charge.

Alarms

Alarms are available which emit a loud emergency siren if the wearer does not move regularly. They are therefore triggered if the wearer is knocked unconscious. They are only effective if someone is within hearing range of the alarm.

First aid:

- take a first-aid kit with you
- if you habitually work alone, attend a first-aid course.

29.1 Dealing with Hazards

As soon as you arrive on site, find out:

- about the site safety organisation and who the site safety supervisors are
- exactly who you report to, and who and what you are responsible for
- how to report hazards which are beyond your control
- where to get further advice
- what personal protective equipment you are required to use, when and where
- where the first-aid room is and who the first aiders are
- fire precaution and emergency procedures and services
- bomb warning contingency plans.

Think ahead. Anticipate the safety issues you will face and know the contingency plans including emergency plans.

Read the site notices and act upon them when necessary.

From time to time you will encounter unsafe conditions or unsafe actions. What can you do about them?

Eliminate or reduce hazards for example by:

- reporting unsafe practices
- reporting unsafe workplaces
- suggesting alternative means of safer construction
- taking action to stop unsafe activities until the situation has been made safe.

Eliminate or reduce risks for example by:

- wearing appropriate protective clothing and safety equipment
- obeying warning signs and notices
- not putting yourself at risk, even if others are in danger.

List contacts and telephone numbers for use in emergency:

When facing a dangerous situation you MUST act immediately to prevent injury to anyone in the vicinity.

EMERGENCY AID

1 RECOGNISE A LACK OF OXYGEN

Arising from	May be causing
ELECTRIC SHOCK	UNCONSCIOUSNESS
DROWNING	
POISONING	NOISY OR
HEAD INJURY	NO BREATHING
GASSING etc	ABNORMAL COLOUR

2 ACT AT ONCE

SWITCH OFF ELECTRICITY, GAS etc
ONLY REMOVE CASUALTY TO PREVENT
FURTHER INJURY
SEND SOMEBODY FOR HELP

GET A CLEAR AIRWAY . . .
REMOVE ANY OBSTRUCTION . . . then

TILT
HEAD BACK

LIFT
JAW

BREATHING MAY RESTART . . . IF NOT . . .

3 APPLY RESCUE BREATHING

START WITH FOUR
QUICK DEEP BREATHS

SEAL NOSE AND
BLOW INTO MOUTH

or

SEAL MOUTH AND
BLOW INTO NOSE

KEEP FINGERS ON JAW
BUT CLEAR OF THROAT

MAINTAIN HEAD
POSITION

AFTER BLOWING INTO
MOUTH or NOSE
WATCH CASUALTY'S
CHEST FALL AS
YOU BREATHE IN

REPEAT EVERY 5 SECS

**AFTER FIRST FOUR
BREATHS TEST FOR
RECOVERY SIGNS**
1. PULSE PRESENT?
2. PUPILS LESS LARGE?
3. COLOUR IMPROVED?   **PULSE POINTS**

4 IF NONE, COMBINE RESCUE BREATHING & HEART COMPRESSION

PLACE CASUALTY
ON A FIRM SURFACE

COMMENCE
HEART COMPRESSION

HEEL OF HAND ONLY
ON LOWER HALF OF
BREASTBONE,
OTHER HAND ON TOP
(FINGERS OFF CHEST)

BREASTBONE

HEART

KEEP ARMS STRAIGHT
AND ROCK FORWARD
TO DEPRESS CHEST
40mm

APPLY 15
COMPRESSIONS ONE
PER SECOND . . . then
GIVE TWO BREATHS

RE-CHECK PULSE . . .
IF STILL ABSENT
CONTINUE WITH
15 COMPRESSIONS
TO TWO BREATHS

IF PULSE RETURNS
CEASE COMPRESSIONS
BUT CONTINUE
RESCUE BREATHING

Rescuers should not put themselves in danger. Another casualty often reduces the chance of providing rapid assistance to the first injured person.

Should an accident occur, follow these rules:

- send for a first aider and/or doctor or ambulance
- separate the cause and the victim if possible, eg switch off electricity supplies, turn off powered plant before assisting the casualty
- move a casualty only to prevent further injury
- check the heart and breathing; give emergency aid as necessary
- stop any bleeding; raise the injured part and apply pressure
- keep the victim warm and reassured
- take care not to become a casualty yourself
- do not remove evidence
- tell your manager.

First aid

First-aiders must be readily identifiable – preferably by wearing a distinctive safety helmet. Ensure you know the first aiders on your site.

You should consider taking a first-aid course. Not only would you learn how to relieve the suffering of an injured colleague, it would help you to stay calm and in control when an accident happens on your site.

The Reporting of Injuries, Diseases and Dangerous Occurrence Regulations (RIDDOR) require some accidents to be reported immediately by telephone to the local HSE office, and others within 7 days using form F28508 or F2508A. Find out whose job it is to do this on your site. It could be yours!

31.1 Accident Investigation

Note all the facts immediately and add these records to your detailed site diary.

If you were a witness or had any responsibility for the work being undertaken when the accident took place you will be required to submit a written report.

Accident investigation has many benefits, including:

- identifying the underlying basic causes
- prevention of recurrence of similar accidents
- identification of training needs
- provision of information in case of litigation.

An accident investigation will usually be done by:

- the senior site manager
- the company safety adviser
- an HSE inspector may be involved.

You may be asked to help their investigation by providing factual information and possibly your opinion.

HSE Inspectors have powers to require the accident location to remain untouched.

The investigation by the HSE Inspector may lead to criminal proceedings. You may be required to give evidence and your report may be used by the Inspectorate and by your company to help establish the cause of the accident. Remember it is an offence to lie or to cover up the facts.

To help you prepare your report, if you witness an accident or are nearby when an accident occurs or had any element of managerial control over the work:

- take immediate notes of what you saw and heard

- make sketches of the accident location

- if appropriate, take photographs of the scene and any relevant detail eg. a broken piece of equipment or a missing guardrail. Consider other people's feelings and explain what you are doing

- identify witnesses who actually saw the accident happen – not just those who were present when the accident occurred

- separate fact from hearsay

- identify and inspect and put aside tools, equipment and materials being used by the injured person(s) at the time of the accident

- check if the work involved a written method statement (other than for rescue) and was it being followed?

- after your investigation, leave the scene as undisturbed as possible.

Your report will be added to your firm's accident/injury records and provide useful information for future training programmes, accident prevention measures, and for improving company policy and working arrangements.

32.1 Bibliography

Source Materials

These materials were supplied to the author by the organisations listed in the Acknowledgements. They are not all publicly available:

- Construction Industry Training Board, *Site Safety Simplified*, GE706.
- W.S. Atkins, *Safety Handbook: and Health and Safety Update*, 16 April 1991.
- Balfour Beatty Construction Ltd, *Health and Safety Update*, Rev. 1991.
- Building Employers Confederation, *Construction Safety*, December 1990
- Costain Group Plc, *Health and Safety Procedures*, January 1991.
- Institution of Civil Engineers, *Construction Safety Handbook*.
- Royal Institution of Chartered Surveyors, *Surveying Safely*, April 1991.
- HMSO, *Safer Road Works Ahead*.
- Health and Safety Executive, *Health and Safety Explained*, August 1989.
- Health and Safety Executive, *Safer Working in Tunnelling*, August 1989.
- Travers Morgan H&S, *Group Health and Safety Manual*, 1991.
- Ove Arup Partnership, *Arup Site Safety Handbook*, February 1990.
- Health and Safety Executive, *Safety in Roofwork*, HSG33 - 9/78.
- Thames Water Utilities Ltd, *Site Safety*, SPD F13.

Bibliography 32.2

This bibliography lists publications that the author referred to in preparing the handbook in addition to the source materials listed opposite. Readers should be aware that some of these publications are updated from time to time and should check that they have the most recent edition.

General
- CITB GE700, *Construction Site Safety Course, Safety Notes*, 1992.
- CONIAC, *Managing Health and Safety in Construction:* Principles and Application to Main Contractor/Sub-Contractor Projects, HSC 1987.
- HSC, Annual Report 1990/91.
- RoSPA 1S 13, *Construction Regulations Handbook* (13th Edition).
- HSC CD43, *Proposals for Workplace (Health, Safety and Welfare) Regulations and Approved Code of Practice*, 1992.
- HSE. *Successful Health and Safety Management*, 1992.

Chapter 1
- HSE SS1, *Construction Summary Sheet, General Legal Requirements*, 1988.
- HSE IND(G) 103(2), *It's Your Job to Manage Safety*, 1991.
- CONIAC, *Guidance on the Implementation of Safety Policies for the Construction Industry*, 1987.

Chapter 2
- CITB FTR 007A, Safety Check Card.

Chapter 3
- HSC CD38, *Personal Protection Equipment at Work Proposals for Regulation and Guidance*, 1991.
- HSE, *Construction (Head Protection) Regulations*, 1986 Guidance on Regulations.

32.3 Bibliography

Chapter 5

- HSE SS11, *Construction Summary Sheet, Safe Use of Propane and Other LPG Cylinders*, 1988.
- HSE CS46, *The Storage and Use of LPG on Construction Sites*, 1981.
- HSE CS4, *The Keeping of LPG in Cylinders and Similar Containers*, 1986.
- HSE HS(R)24, *A Guide to the Road Traffic (Carriage of Dangerous Substances in Packages etc.) Regulations*, 1986.

Chapter 6

- HSE EXL5, *Maintain Buildings Safety*, 1988.
- HSE HS(G)58, *Evaluation and Inspection of Buildings and Structures*, 1990.

Chapter 7

- HSE EH40/92, *Occupational Exposure Limits*, 1992.
- HSC COP3, *Work with Asbestos Insulation, Asbestos Coating and Asbestos Board*, 1988.
- HSC, *Control of Lead at Work*, 1985.
- CONIAC, *Hazard Information Sheet 1, Cement*, 1985.
- Cleveland County Council, *Diamonds are for Danger.*
- HSE MS(B)9, *Save Your Skin*, 1990.
- HSE EH47, *The Provision, Use and Maintenance of Hygiene Facilities for Work with Asbestos Insulation and Coatings*, 1990.
- CIRIA, *A guide to the control of substances hazardous to health in design and construction*, Report 125, 1992.

Chapter 8

- CFL Vision, *Watch that Space,* (Video).
- HSE SS15, *Construction Summary Sheet, Confined Spaces*, 1988.
- HSE GS5, *Entry into Confined Spaces*, 1980.

Chapter 9
- CITB, *Mobile Crane Operators Safety Guide*, 1979.
- HSE SS13, *Construction Summary Sheet, Construction Goods Hoists*, 1988.
- HSE, *Construction Sheet No. 19, Safe Use of Mobile Cranes on Construction Sites*, 1991
- HSE PM42, *Excavators Used as Cranes*, 1984.

Chapter 10
- HSE GS29, *Health and Safety in Demolition Work*, 1985 (in four parts).

Chapter 11
- Yorkshire Electricity, *Prevention of Accidents; Building and Construction*, 1991.
- HSE SS6, *Construction Summary Sheet, Portable Electric Tools and Equipment*, 1988.
- HSE GS24, *Electricity on Construction Sites*, 1983.

Chapter 12
- CIRIA Technical Note 95, *Proprietary Trench Support Systems*, E.B. Mackay, 1986 (3rd Edition) reprint pending.
- CIRIA Report 97, *Trenching Practice*, D.J. Irvine & R.J.H. Smith, 1992 (4th Edition).
- HSE SS8, *Construction Summary Sheet, Safety in Excavations*, 1988.

Chapter 13
- HSC HS(G)33, *Safety in Roof work*, 1987.
- HSE IND(G) 21(L), *Working on Fragile Roofs*, 1989.
- HSE GS10, *Roof Work: Prevention of Falls*, 1979.
- HSE, *Deadly Maintenance – Roofs – A Study of Fatal Accidents at Work*, 1985.

32.5 Bibliography

Chapter 14
- HSE, *Flammable Liquids on Construction Sites*, 1988.
- HSE, *Fires & Explosives Due to Misuse of Oxygen*, 1987.
- HSE, *Highly Flammable Materials on Construction Sites*, 1978.

Chapter 15
- HSE LS28, *Safe Erection of Structures*, 1984 (in 4 parts).
- BCSA 20/89, *Structural Steelwork Erection*, W.H. Arch 1989.

Chapter 16
- HSC CD36, *Manual Handling of Loads, Proposals for Regulations and Guidance*, 1991.
- HSE, *Agricultural Safety Leaflet – Lifting and Carrying*, 1988.

Chapter 17
- BS 5228 : Part 1 : 1984, *Noise Control on Reconstruction and Open Sites* – Part 1.
- CIRIA Technical Note 138, *Planning to Reduce Noise Exposure in Construction*. R.A. Waller 1990
- CONIAC, *Health Hazard Information Sheet, Noise*, 1986.
- HSE IND(G) 99(L), *Noise at Work – Advice for Employees*, 1991.
- HSE, *Noise at Work, Noise Guides 1/2 and 3 to 8*, 1989.

Chapter 18
- HSE GS4, *Safety in Pressure Testing*, 1977.
- CPDA, *Testing of Drains and Sewers, Water and Air Tests*, 1981.

Chapter 19
- HSE GS7, *Accidents to Children on Construction Sites*, 1977.

Chapter 20
- HSE SS10, *Construction Summary Sheet, Tower Scaffolds*, 1988.
- HSE SS3, *Construction Summary Sheet, General Access Scaffolds*, 1988.
- CITB, CE509, *A Guide to Practical Scaffolding*, 1987.
- HSE GS15, *General Access Scaffolds*, 1982.
- HSE GS42, *Tower Scaffolds*, 1987.

Chapter 21
- British Drilling Association, *Guidance Notes for the Safe Drilling of Landfills and Contaminated Land*, 1992.
- Scott Wilson Kirkpatrick, *Site Safety for Ground Investigation Staff*, 1992.

Chapter 23
- Forestry Safety Council, *The Chain Saw*, 1977.
- CITB GE704, *Safety in the Use of Woodworking Machines*, 1989.
- CITB GE703, *Saw Site Safety*, 1989.
- HSE IND(G) 16(C), *Safe Working with Small Dumpers*.

Chapter 24
- HSE, *Final Report of the Advisory Committee On Falsework*, 1975.

Chapter 25
- HSE IND(G) 31(L), *Danger! Transport at Work*, 1985.

Chapter 26
- HMSO, *Traffic Signs Manual, Chapter 8 Volumes 1 and 2*, 1991.

32.7 Bibliography

Chapter 28
- RICS, *Surveying Safety – A Personal Commitment.*
- HSE IND(G) 73(L), *Working along in Safety*, 1990.

Chapter 30
- HSC, *First Aid at Work. Health and Safety (First Aid) Regulations 1981 and Guidance. Approved Code of Practice*, 1990.
- HSE 11, *Reporting on Injury on a Dangerous Occurrence*, 1990.

Chapter 31
- HSE IND(G) 113L, *Your Firm's Injury Rates and How to Use Them*, 1991.

Free publications:

For literature and information about free HSE publications contact the HSE public enquiry point:

HSE
Broad Lane
Sheffield
S3 7HQ
Tel: 0742 892345 or 892346
Fax: 0742 720006.

Priced publications:

All priced HSE publications are available from HMSO.

All HSE current publications are listed in "Publication In Series: List of HSC/HSE Publications", which is updated regularly and is available free from the HSE public enquiry point.

Report forms:

Until early 1992 HMSO published a number of forms for recording the results of examinations and tests of lifting equipment and plant and for specifying safe working loads. These forms summarised the information prescribed under the various Regulations in a convenient format.

The forms are no longer available from HMSO, but where companies have stocks of the original they may still be used. Copies of forms F54, 75, 80, 87, 88, 91, 96, 97 and 2040 may still be made and used.

Subject Index

Subject Index

Subject Index

Subject Index

Core Programme Members
(July 1993)

Consultants

ACER Consultants Ltd
Ove Arup Partnership
W S Atkins Consultants Limited
Babtie Group Ltd
Binnie & Partners
Building Design Partnership
Brian Colquhoun & Partners
Sir Alexander Gibb & Partners Limited
Frank Graham Group Limited
Sir William Halcrow & Partners Ltd
G Maunsell & Partners
Montgomery Watson Ltd
Mott MacDonald Group Ltd
L G Mouchel & Partners Ltd
Posford Duvivier
Rendel Palmer & Tritton
Rofe Kennard & Lapworth
Scott Wilson Kirkpatrick & Partners
Wardell Armstrong
Sir Owen Williams and Partners
  Geotechnical Ltd

Water Utilities

Northumbrian Water Limited
North West Water Limited
South West Water Services Ltd
Southern Water Services Ltd
Thames Water Utilities Ltd
Wessex Water plc
Yorkshire Water Services Ltd

Contractors

AMEC p.l.c.
Balfour Beatty Ltd
Henry Boot & Sons PLC
Galliford plc
Higgs & Hill Construction Holdings Ltd
Kyle Stewart Design Services Ltd
Laing Technology Group Ltd
Alfred McAlpine Construction Ltd
Miller Civil Engineering Ltd
Edmund Nuttall Limited
Tarmac Construction Ltd
Taylor Woodrow Construction Holdings Ltd
Trafalgar House Technology
Willmott Dixon Ltd
George Wimpey PLC

Others

British Telecom
Cementitious Slag Makers Association
Department of the Environment
Department of Transport
Health & Safety Executive
Hong Kong Government Secretariat
H R Wallingford Ltd
ICI Engineering
Institution of Civil Engineers
London Underground Limited
National Power
National Rivers Authority
PSA Projects Limited
Scottish Hydro-Electric plc
Union Railways Limited